Dedication

I am dedicating this to my children; George, Annalyse, Adam, Sean, Marcus, Alex, Victor II, Brian, and Jordyn; my husband, Victor; my grandchildren Anastaysia, Nataliya, Caius, Atlas, and Jenavieve; my parents, Mark Gould and late Phyllis Mosley Gould Carter and my Grandmothers, the late Marion Gould, and Rebecca Loatman Mosley Seeney.

Imprint: Independently published

ISBN: 978-1-969075-08-7

www.TyGouldJacinto.com

Tyrese Gould Jacinto

Illustrations by Arnild C. Aldepolla

TWENTY TWENTY-ONE

Unlock Your Blessings

20 ways to unlock blessings to practice for 21 days.

Contents

Introduction

Many books and sages explain how to achieve health, wealth, and peace of mind. But I find there are very few materials to help with the process and maintain the results successfully.

This method, although simple, will help you with training and meditation. This is a scientific approach that I use successfully for health, wealth, and peace of mind.

This method is the twenty-one-day practice method. Practice a virtue for the entire 21 days, then meditate on your success for the remaining 7 days. This is the best way to form a habit, good or bad.

I will even start this on the new moon to follow the 28-day moon cycle. You will need a simple calendar to keep track of the days.

It is a coincidence that I decided to publish this in 2021. There are 20 main virtues to practice for 21 days. What a great time to be awake!

Affirmation to repeat daily:

"Thank you, Lord, for this new day and all the blessings that came my way" - *Tyrese Gould Jacinto*

First Key to Unlock Your Blessing…

Do not complain about anything.

Constant complaining will rewire your brain to cause future complaining. Eventually, it will be easier to complain than to be positive, regardless of the blessings you achieve.

Complaining will ultimately become a significant part of your behavior, changing how people react to you.

The stress caused by complaining will have a lasting and negative impact on your brain. A few days of stress can damage the neurons in the brain used for problem-solving and reasoning. Complaining will impair the brain's ability to create new neurons to attract blessings.

Complaining will block your ability to see opportunities that lead to your ultimate purpose. You use affirmations, meditation, and various other methods; however, complaining will block the sensory receptors. You will miss the subtle glimpses of light that will lead you to your path to success.

Without complaining, you will be happy and satisfied, experiencing joy and thankfulness. For the next 21 days, conscientiously concentrate on your mental state.

Do not complain for 21 days. When the 21 days are over, meditate for the next 7 days on the entire 3 weeks to determine how you felt each day.

When you discern that you no longer need to complain, you will feel a sense of weightlessness.

Author's Follow-Up (Reflection)

Years after writing these words, I have come to understand that releasing complaint is not a single activity; it is a continual spiritual practice. What began as a 21-day experiment became a way of life. I learned that every sigh, every subtle thought of resistance, carried the same energy as complaint. The moment I recognized this, something within me softened. I began to move through life with a quieter heart and clearer mind.

Without the habit of complaint, I found myself responding to challenges with calm rather than frustration. Tasks that once felt burdensome became opportunities to give thanks and stay present. The mind became lighter, and blessings began to flow naturally, without force or striving.

I discovered that gratitude is not simply the opposite of complaint; it is a sacred awareness that transforms ordinary moments into gifts. Through consistent practice, I felt closer to the Creator, grounded in peace, and aligned with purpose. Living without complaint revealed a more profound truth: that joy is not found by changing the world around us, but by changing the way we see it.

Second Key to Unlock Your Blessing…

Remove the concept of fail.

To fail has never been a word that any generation has used in our existence. To fail is to admit that the Creator is not in charge, and we have no faith in the path of our existence. We must walk that path and take action.

When the Creator and Nature guide our paths, we can recognize what we are responsible for.

Some journeys are short and some are very long. Like the pages in a book, they only go from cover to cover. However, it is as we turn the page and close the book.

As long as we wake each day, we learn something new. One new thought or encounter moves us closer to our destiny that has been started for us by only the Creator.

To say that we have failed is to admit that the Great Spirit does not govern our lives.

Indigenous people are not competitive; therefore, we do not know failure. We have goals that are only for ourselves and never to compare or compete with others. When we compete, there will always be winners and losers or successes and failures.

Competitions will keep us on the forever swing of the pendulum that never ceases to swing in opposite directions.

The equal swing must compensate for the swing to the right, to the left, and so forth. We must stop the swing and keep our eyes on the Creator, and our journeys and paths will be straightforward.

You will be happy and satisfied in a state of joy and thankfulness. For the next 21 days, conscientiously remove the concept of fail from your mental state. Analyze each experience for 21 days. When the 21 days are over, meditate for the next 7 days on the entire 3 weeks to determine how you felt each day.

When you discern that you no longer fail, you will feel a sense of weightlessness.

Author's Follow-Up (Reflection)

Years after first writing about removing the concept of fail, I have come to see this truth even more clearly through experience. Life has continued to reveal that what we often call "failure" is simply the Creator's redirection, a sacred turn in the path that teaches humility, patience, and faith. When I stopped labeling experiences as failures, I began to notice the perfection woven into what once felt like disappointment. Each challenge was a lesson in disguise, preparing me for blessings that required a stronger, wiser spirit.

Living without the word fail has freed my heart from the weight of comparison. I no longer measure progress by what others achieve, but by how closely I walk with purpose and truth. In this practice, I have learned that the Great Spirit never wastes a moment. Even the pauses, the closed doors, and the detours have meaning.

By trusting the Creator's design, I found peace in knowing that nothing is ever truly lost. Every experience carries wisdom, and every ending opens the door to a greater beginning. To remove the concept of failure is to walk in harmony with life itself, accepting that all things, even the most challenging moments, serve the unfolding of our destiny.

Third Key to Unlock Your Blessing…

Consciously have no opinions.

Opinions, we can be peaceful without them.
What would happen if we consciously decided not to have any opinions?

In many instances, our opinions distract from our goals. We waste our time and energy, which causes delays in our blessings. When we cease opinions, we can release ourselves from the grip of social pressures and cares. Lack of opinions offers peace of mind when you embrace reality as it is, without the need to argue and engage in needless negative comments.

Most opinions we form are based on a limited set of facts and information. Do our opinions matter? How do they improve our state of mind or lives?

Our lives would be peaceful, our relationships more substantial, and our actions more productive if we ceased to comment on everything. An opinion is an expression of our perspective on any given issue or situation, and not facts. They are an expression of a point of view.

Opinions are not actions. We rarely act after expressing an opinion, which is counterproductive. If an issue is important to us, we can make the right move. Not having an opinion is about awareness of what's important and what we can do.

Instead of creating more conflict in the world and adding to our stress, we can choose peace of mind. We can replace opinions with calm reflection and focus on how we can live our lives.

And when we have a view about something important, we can choose quiet action over loud, empty opinions.

You will be happy and satisfied in a state of joy and thankfulness. For the next 21 days, conscientiously be silent in your thinking of opinions in your mental state. Analyze each experience for 21 days.

When the 21 days are over, meditate for the next 7 days on the entire 3 weeks to determine how you felt each day.

When you discern that you no longer need to form an opinion, you will feel a sense of weightlessness.

Author's Follow-Up (Reflection)

Several years after practicing the art of having no opinions, I have found a peace that cannot be described in words. At first, silence meant withholding thoughts, but I soon learned it meant releasing the need to define everything. In the stillness beyond opinions, the mind quiets and the heart awakens. I began to listen more deeply, to people, to nature, and to the subtle guidance of the Creator.

By no longer reacting to every situation with judgment or commentary, I discovered freedom. My energy, once scattered by endless thoughts and debates, became focused and calm. Relationships softened; conversations became more meaningful. I noticed that when I stopped trying to be right, harmony naturally followed. The absence of opinion created space for understanding and compassion.

Through this practice, I found that truth reveals itself without my interference. Life continues perfectly on its own without my commentary. The Creator's design needs no approval. Living without opinions opened my spirit to gratitude for simply being. It taught me that peace is not found through control or expression, but through surrender and awareness. In silence, I found the purest connection to joy, and in joy, the blessing of complete contentment.

Fourth Key to Unlock Your Blessing…

First, help others to succeed.

This concept is foreign to some, yet its principles date back to some of the oldest teachings, and we still have access to them.

The Bible is one of the most familiar with the famous verse, "Give and it shall be given unto you." I will not elaborate, but I will provide more details on how this powerful experience will undoubtedly unlock your blessings.

The profound realization when you focus on others first is that you are not focused on yourself. When we focus on ourselves first, our thoughts could jeopardize the thought process with feelings of lack or the desire to have without faith. Focusing on ourselves can block the thought process and hide opportunities due to our overwhelming sense that we must have it.

Pray and have faith is by no means, pray and dwell. I like to say that I "set it and forget it." This is faith that my prayers will come to fruition, and I can stay focused on the light that leads my path.

When we help others first, we open the floodgates to many blessings. We are meant to be dedicated to helping those who need and ask. We all have talents, skills, knowledge, and wisdom for the Creator's use through us as spiritual beings having a human experience. We are all one, and when one lacks or is lost, none can rest and have peace.

I know that this will be difficult for some, but I encourage everyone to focus on others first. Remember your experiences as you practice and keep them up to become a fiber of your being.

You will be happy and satisfied in a state of joy and thankfulness. For the next 21 days, conscientiously help others first. Focus on the needs of others you encounter. Analyze each experience for 21 days.

When the 21 days are over, meditate for the next 7 days on the entire 3 weeks to determine how you felt each day.

When you discern that your needs will also be met and your dreams and prayers come true, you will feel a sense of weightlessness.

Author's Follow-Up (Reflection)

Years after practicing the principle of helping others first, I have witnessed the profound truth that giving is the key that opens every door. What began as a conscious effort has become a natural rhythm of life. Each time I placed someone else's success before my own, I felt the quiet assurance of divine balance, as if the Creator was saying, "You are cared for because you care for others."

Helping others shifted my focus from lack to abundance. I began to see that my gifts were not meant to be stored but shared. The more I gave time, encouragement, or knowledge, the more space for blessings to flow back into my life. Opportunities appeared effortlessly, and what once seemed distant came closer with ease.

This practice revealed a sacred harmony: we rise by lifting others. The moment we release the fear of not having enough, we step into the Creator's flow of infinite provision. Today, I no longer measure success by what I achieve alone, but by how many hearts I help awaken to their own light. Serving others has become my joy, my peace, and my greatest blessing. In giving, I discovered that I was never lacking, only waiting to overflow.

Fifth Key to Unlock Your Blessing…

Cease hatred.

Hatred is an emotion that arises from being betrayed or hurt physically or emotionally by someone. Feeling hatred, no matter how long, will cause harm to the spirit, mind, and body.

Hate attracts negative emotions, affects your relationships, blocks your blessings, and causes you mental blindness to your path to success. Experiencing hatred changes the chemistry in your brain. When you hate, you can become aggressive while feeling hateful to fight or flee.

Hatred will negatively impact your immune system, your endocrine system, and your nervous system. Your Extreme emotions will cause you to release stress hormones in your brain. The stress from your hate releases hormones that cause inflammation throughout the body, leading to significant health consequences. You will have low energy and feel tired from the tension that hate causes in your physical body.

When you feel a sense of hate, quickly get to the root cause of the feeling. This will help you promptly dispel any emotional damage to your spirit and body.

Cease hatred, and you will be happy and satisfied in a state of joy and thankfulness. For the next 21 days, cease hate.

Focus on what caused the feeling and dispel the emotion. Analyze each experience for 21 days.

When the 21 days are over, meditate for the next 7 days on the entire 3 weeks to determine how you felt each day.

When you discern that you no longer feel the emotion of hate, you will feel a sense of weightlessness.

Author's Follow-Up (Reflection)

Years of practicing the release of hatred have taught me that forgiveness is the highest form of freedom. Hatred once felt justified as a defense against pain or betrayal, but I learned that it only chained me to the past. Even subtle resentment or disappointment carried the same heavy energy. When I chose to release it, peace began to take root.

As I let go, I noticed my body respond: my breath deepened, my sleep improved, and my spirit felt lighter. The mind can heal when the heart no longer clings to anger. Hatred had never punished those who hurt me; it only drained my own strength.

Through this practice, I found compassion for those lost in their own suffering. The act of ceasing hate is not weakness; it is sacred courage. It restores harmony within and around us. Once the bitterness dissolved, blessings flowed easily again. The Creator's love cannot dwell in a heart filled with anger. Living without hatred, I discovered that peace is not something we find; it is something we uncover once we stop resisting love.

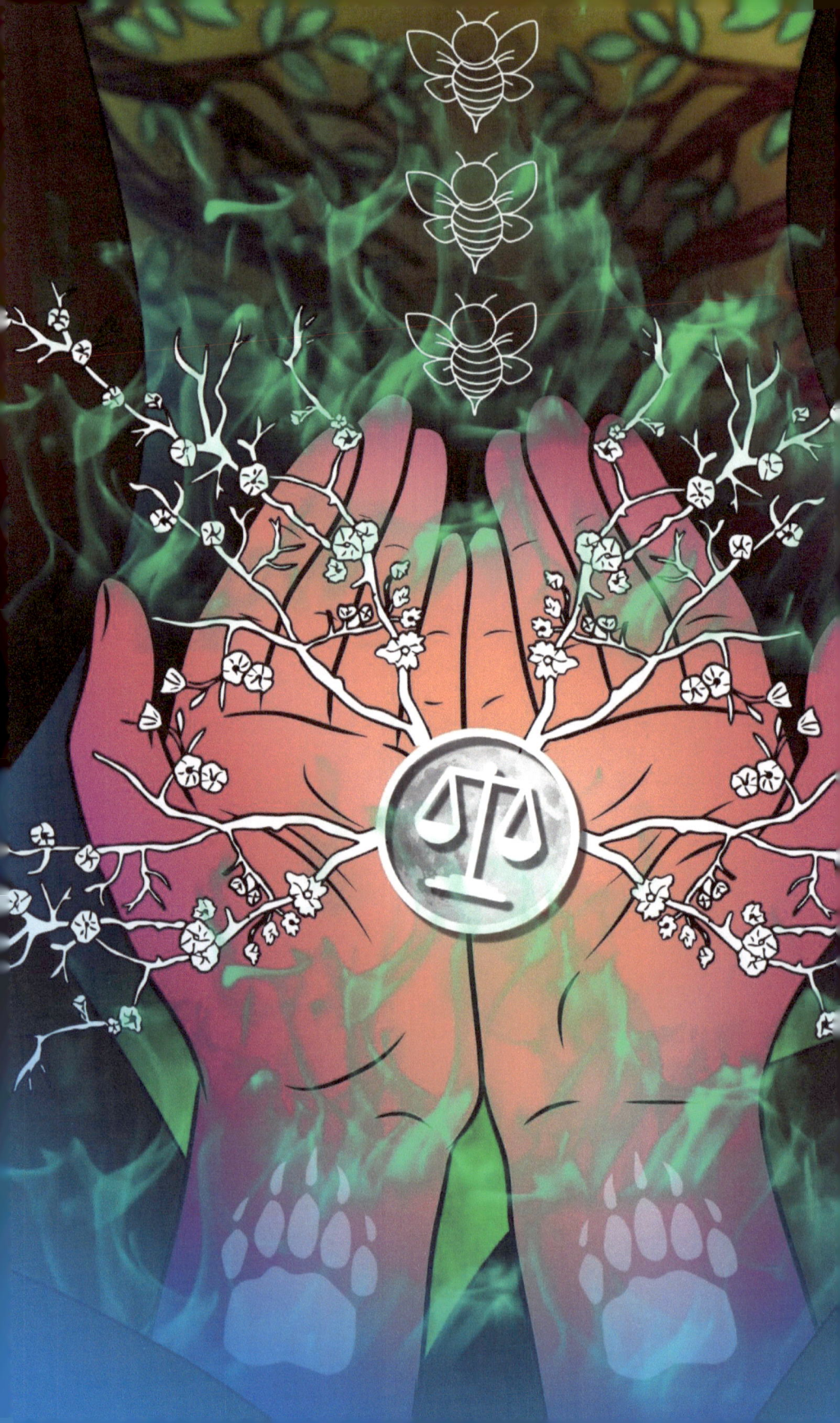

Sixth Key to Unlock Your Blessing…

Always do the right thing.

Choosing to do the right thing when you have a choice of actions is essential for well-being. Do the right thing despite possible consequences and treat others rightly.

If you do the right thing, you will not feel guilty for doing something you should not have done. When you practice righteousness, you are free from guilt and fear. Doing wrong will bring about fear of judgment and rejection.

Doing the right thing always leads to transparency and more right actions. Engaging in the wrong activities will lead to more situations resulting from the original immoral act.

When you are in righteousness, your light will shine bright, your conscience will be free, your disposition and attitude will be pleasant, and you will undoubtedly open the door to blessings. If you do wrong, your negative emotions will block any good that could surround you.

You must be in the right to see the light on the right path to your success.

You will be happy and satisfied in a state of joy and thankfulness.

For the next 21 days, do the right thing regardless of the situation. Be aware of the decisions that you make. Analyze each experience for 21 days.

When the 21 days are over, meditate for the next 7 days on the entire 3 weeks to determine how you felt each day.

When you discern that you can be righteous, you will feel a sense of weightlessness.

Author's Follow-Up (Reflection)

Time and experience have revealed that doing the right thing is not always the easiest path, but it is always the most freeing. I have faced moments when truth and convenience stood at opposite ends, and choosing righteousness required courage, humility, and patience. Yet every time I decided integrity over impulse, peace followed.

Doing the right thing has become more than a moral practice; it is a spiritual alignment. When my actions harmonize with my higher self, I feel connected to the Creator and the natural order of life. I've learned that even when others misunderstand or oppose your choices, right action carries its own quiet reward: the absence of inner conflict.

There is a strength in staying true to your spirit when the world tests your light. Right living builds trust in yourself and faith in the unseen. The more I honor truth, the lighter my heart becomes, and the blessings flow naturally because goodness is a magnet for grace.

Seventh Key to Unlock Your Blessing…

Go above and beyond.

Going above and beyond has many layers of blessings. We find this concept in our ancient teachings, and the benefits to your life are incredible.

Some of the more famous teachings include the Bible's mention that you reap what you sow. The seeds we plant now will grow to be what we sow. The same is true in that we cannot harvest if we do not plant any seeds.

Each time you act, you are planting tiny seeds toward your blessings. This will open your senses to opportunities for reaching your goals. Do not expect to achieve blessings in life if you are not going above and beyond.

The life you lead and your actions will fuel your future events, which are direct results of your past. We need to work hard in our lives to realize our blessings.

Going above and beyond leads us to the fruits of our Spirit, within which are: love, peace, patience, joy, kindness, goodness, faithfulness, gentleness, and self-control (Galatians 5:22).

When we go above and beyond, we sow this in our lives, and good things are the result. Going above and beyond will lead to faith, and the blessings will unite us with the Creator. Blessings will lead you to the power of the Spirit.

You will be happy and satisfied in a state of joy and thankfulness.

For the next 21 days, go above and beyond regardless of the situation. Be aware of the decisions that you make. Analyze each experience for 21 days.

When the 21 days are over, meditate for the next 7 days on the entire 3 weeks to determine how you felt each day.

When you discern that you go above and beyond, you will feel a sense of weightlessness.

Author's Follow-Up (Reflection)

In this season of my journey, "going above and beyond" has deepened into a sacred act of devotion. It is no longer just about effort; it is about intention. When I give from the heart, without expectation of return, I align myself with the rhythm of creation. The blessings that follow are not always material; sometimes, they come as peace, clarity, or unexpected guidance.

Going beyond what is required opens the doorway to divine reciprocity. The Creator sees the sincerity behind our actions, not the size of them. Each extra step, each moment of compassion, each unseen act of love plants a seed that blooms in time.

There were moments when I felt weary and wondered if my giving mattered. Yet every time I stayed the course, I found renewal in spirit. To go above and beyond is to live with faith to trust that what we offer will return multiplied in beauty and purpose.

Through this, I have learned that the greatest blessing is not in what we receive, but in who we become when we give our all.

Eighth Key to Unlock Your Blessing…

Have a positive attitude.

The floodgates of blessings will flow with a consistent positive attitude. Being positive will help you consciously and subconsciously. This blocks negative thoughts, concerns, and doubts.

When you have a positive attitude, your blessings will blossom. Your brain will begin to operate in a state of bliss with free-flowing feel-good hormones called endorphins, which are beneficial for you and allow you to be happier.

Your positive attitude will boost your confidence, making you feel more adept and aware of the blessings that might have previously been outside your reach.

With a positive mental attitude, you will see the valuable lesson in every situation, good or bad. You will be able to discern the cause and take control of your emotions by practicing turning them around into positive thinking.

When you practice maintaining a positive attitude toward yourself, the people around you will be blessed along with you.

Having a positive attitude is likened to counting your blessings. Clearly state what you are thankful for. Affirm that everything is as it should be and that all blessings are coming your way. You will quickly find out that any negative thoughts will disappear.

A positive attitude will undoubtedly open the way for blessings to reveal themselves, and opportunities will manifest where you thought that none existed.

You will be happy and satisfied in a state of joy and thankfulness.

For the next 21 days, have a positive attitude regardless of the situation. Be aware of the reactions you have. Analyze each experience for 21 days.

When the 21 days are over, meditate for the next 7 days on the entire 3 weeks to determine how you felt each day.

When you discern that you will maintain a positive attitude, you will feel a sense of weightlessness.

Author's Follow-Up (Reflection)

Maintaining a positive attitude has become my daily act of faith. It is not about denying reality; it is about choosing the higher vibration of truth. Every day brings situations that could easily shift us toward doubt or frustration. Still, when I remain grounded in gratitude, I rise above the noise.

I've learned that positivity is power. It doesn't come from pretending everything is perfect; it comes from trusting that everything serves a divine purpose. When I wake each morning with a thankful heart, I notice how easily blessings unfold. The smallest acts, a smile, a kind word, or a peaceful response, carry transformative energy.

Positivity has also made me a mirror for others. When I choose joy, those around me feel it and respond in kind. This exchange of light uplifts entire spaces and communities.

A positive attitude opens the heart to receive and the spirit to create. The more I practice it, the more life itself becomes a reflection of faith in motion. Through it, I've discovered that joy is not found, it is made, moment by moment, in alignment with gratitude and love.

Ninth Key to Unlock Your Blessing…

Listen more.

Listening more is an act of love. When you hear, you are considering the other person and their statements. Good listening will lead you to ask questions to get to know a person better.

When you listen wholeheartedly, you can discern what makes a person and their life experiences unique, and you will learn something valuable that may unlock your blessings. "Know this, my beloved brothers: let every person be quick to hear, slow to speak, slow to anger" (James 1:19).

When you listen, pay attention to the entire story before asking any questions. Take a moment to show that you care and ponder before you respond. Listening more will show the person that you care, and the energy between you will be peaceful and vibrant.

There may be some similarities; however, do not overtalk the person you are listening to. Allow that person to finish and ask you questions. If the person does not ask, do not offer your like stories. Your blessings will come in the silence and attentiveness that you give before you are asked to comment.

Listen more; there may be a time when it is your turn to speak, but only when approached to do so.

Do not listen to someone negative, perverse, wicked, or who curses. Words are magical sound frequencies from the Creator to help in the spiritual realm. Know when to draw the line and use common sense.

Poor listening diminishes another person, and good listening requires concentration. Fools find no pleasure in understanding but delight in airing their own opinions. Proverbs 18:2.

After listening more, you can ask detailed, open-ended questions that don't result in merely yes or no answers but gently peek beneath the surface, without prying into details the person does not want to share.

You will be happy and satisfied in a state of joy and thankfulness.

For the next 21 days, listen more and speak less. Be aware of the feelings you have. Analyze each experience for 21 days. When the 21 days are over, meditate for the next 7 days on the entire 3 weeks to determine how you felt each day.

When you listen more, you will feel a sense of weightlessness.

Author's Follow-Up (Reflection)

Listening has become one of my most excellent teachers. Over time, I have learned that listening is not about waiting for my turn to speak; it is about entering sacred silence where wisdom resides. Authentic listening connects the heart to the spirit of another and reveals divine messages hidden in ordinary words.

When I began practicing deep listening, I noticed how peaceful my surroundings became. Conflicts faded, relationships strengthened, and I began to hear the subtle guidance of the Creator more clearly. The act of stillness allows Spirit to move through others, offering lessons I could never have found in my own thoughts.

Listening is also an act of humility. It requires us to surrender our ego, to acknowledge that every person carries a spark of divine truth. When we give that truth space to unfold, we honor creation itself.

Today, I see listening as a pathway to understanding, compassion, and healing. It opens a channel between souls and strengthens our unity as spiritual beings sharing this human experience. The blessing of listening more is that it teaches us to truly hear not only others, but the whisper of the Creator within.

Tenth Key to Unlock Your Blessing…

Forgive and forget.

Forgiveness and forgetting are freeing to the soul, spirit, and body. The act unlocks blessings and opportunities that would otherwise be blocked by the emotions that you alone feel. The feelings caused by not forgiving or forgetting can do harm to your physical body.

The Creator's most extraordinary act is forgiveness. We should do the same to be free, and forgive ourselves our debts, as we also have forgiven our debtors, Matthew 6:12. In verses in Matthew 25 and 26. And when you stand praying, if you hold anything against anyone, forgive them, so that your Father in heaven may forgive you your sins."

When you do not forgive and forget, you find yourself in a state of pain and torment, which can lead to aggravation. You will block any good that comes your way. Unforgiveness blocks the Creator's power, and you will not be able to see the blessings or opportunities. The flow will be stopped.

When you forgive, you break down fear and experience faith.

If you do not forgive and forget, you will injure your soul, spirit, and body with strife. You will be held in bondage by acts beyond your control; however, you now have even more control over yourself than in the original incident. If you hurt someone, you will, in turn, be forgiven just as you have done so. You will be released, and the blessings will flow freely.

You will be happy and satisfied in a state of joy and thankfulness.

For the next 21 days, forgive and forget to receive your forgiveness and blessings. Refuse to remember. Be aware of the feelings you have. Analyze each experience for 21 days.

When the 21 days are over, meditate for the next 7 days on the entire 3 weeks to determine how you felt each day.

When you forgive and forget, you will feel a sense of weightlessness.

Author's Follow-Up (Reflection)

Forgiveness has been one of my most significant spiritual revelations. I have learned that to forgive is not to excuse, but to release the burden that keeps the soul in bondage. The act of forgiveness does not erase the past; it transforms how it lives within us. Forgetting, then, becomes a choice to no longer feed the memory with pain.

When I began to forgive genuinely, I felt a lightness in my being. The energy that once weighed me down turned into peace. I understood that forgiveness is a divine exchange: we give up bitterness and receive freedom in return. The Creator's love flows most freely through a heart unchained by resentment.

Through the years, I have also learned that forgiveness must begin with oneself. We cannot extend what we have not embraced. Each time I forgave myself, I opened new channels of understanding and compassion for others.

To forgive and forget is to align with divine will to allow the Creator's grace to do its healing work. This key continues to unlock blessings in my life by teaching me that peace is not found in remembering wrongs but in remembering love.

Eleventh Key to Unlock Your Blessing…

Have personal initiative.

Blessings happen when you have a personal initiative to seek opportunities to grow, learn, and do good works. We are told to seek first the kingdom, but the key lies in the word seek. Seeking is a personal initiative.

We will not be blessed if we shirk the work that must be done. Procrastination and laziness lead to poverty. We will only find blessings when we seek to complete the tasks revealed to us in faith. Your Personal initiative requires a sense of responsibility to move toward our goals and unlock our blessings. When we take personal initiative, we also find glimpses of light that lead us on the path of righteousness.

"Blessed are those who hear the word of God and observe it" (11:28). This is initiative, and we must do what needs to be done when it should be done, and without murmuring and complaint. We take personal initiative to get up in the morning and go to work. We are dedicated to our families and to the home in which we live.

There is more than just a survival initiative. We must grow, and to grow, we must take personal initiative to seek our blessings. "Let us not lose heart in doing good, for in due time, we will reap if we do not grow weary." "So then, while we have an opportunity, let us do good to all people, and especially to those who are of the household of the faith" (Galatians 6:9-10).

If the Creator did not have initiative, then we would not be here. There would be no animals, plants, or other creatures that we live with.

There are many blessings when you have personal initiative, and only good will come from practicing this most important virtue.

You will be happy and satisfied in a state of joy and thankfulness.

For the next 21 days, have a personal initiative to receive blessings. Be aware of the feelings you have. Analyze each experience for 21 days. When the 21 days are over, meditate for the next 7 days on the entire 3 weeks to determine how you felt each day.

When you have personal initiative, you will feel a sense of weightlessness.

Author's Follow-Up (Reflection)

Over the years, I have witnessed how personal initiative creates divine momentum. It is as if the Creator waits patiently for us to take the first step, and once we do, the universe aligns to meet us halfway. Initiative is faith in motion; it is the silent prayer spoken through action.

Through practice, I discovered that blessings do not simply arrive; they unfold as we move. The smallest act of initiative, a call made, a plan started, a hand extended, can ripple outward, shaping miracles we could not yet see. When I took consistent initiative toward the vision placed in my heart, doors opened with grace, and people appeared as answers to unspoken prayers.

Personal initiative also builds inner strength. It silences doubt, for every completed action whisper, I can. This confidence deepens faith and reinforces the truth that the Creator works through us, not for us.

When initiative becomes a daily habit, blessings multiply naturally. We no longer wait for change; we become the change, guided by divine will. Every moment of motion, no matter how small, carries us closer to purpose. The Creator blesses those who rise and move with faith, for movement itself is a sacred form of prayer.

Twelfth Key to Unlock Your Blessing…

Treat all with justice and loyalty.

Treat all with justice and loyalty, and never deliberately mislead or deceive others by any actions. Be cautious not to use overstatements, half-truths, omissions, or any other methods that would be unjust. You will earn the trust of others through your integrity and consistency with your thoughts, words, and actions. You need your inner strength to do the right thing in all situations.

If you live by these principles, you will be honorable, upright, and truly blessed.

When we demonstrate loyalty, we can make independent decisions that are for the good of all. We will unlock our blessings when we decide to treat others as we wish to be treated.

If we wrong others unjustly and deliberately, we break their loyalty and our own. Have selfless love and concern for others. When you are acting for the benefit of someone else, even when it is undeserved, you are blessed.

We have a righteousness that is internal and deep-seated. This act will genuinely change the way we treat each other and will unlock the blessings.

Be just and loyal in all situations. The blessing will be a result of your commitment to justice and loyalty. Your equal treatment of individuals and tolerance of diversity will lead you to the light of your path.

You will be happy and satisfied in a state of joy and thankfulness.

For the next 21 days, treat all with justice and loyalty. Be aware of the feelings you have. Analyze each experience for 21 days. When the 21 days are over, meditate for the next 7 days on the entire 3 weeks to determine how you felt each day.

When you treat others as you should be treated, you will feel a sense of weightlessness.

Author's Follow-Up (Reflection)

Time has revealed that justice and loyalty are not merely virtues; they are living energies that return to us in unexpected ways. When we choose to act justly, even when it costs us comfort or recognition, we align with divine order. Justice is not about judgment; it is about balance, ensuring that what we give and what we receive are rooted in truth.

In my own walk, I learned that loyalty does not demand agreement; it requires steadfastness. It is the ability to hold space for others even when their path differs from ours. Loyalty to truth, to integrity, and to the Creator's guidance will sustain your spirit through every test.

Living with justice and loyalty has drawn people of honesty and light into my life. These relationships became reflections of the same integrity I chose to uphold. Every moment of fairness, every act of sincerity, opened a doorway to greater peace.

True blessings do not come from how we are treated, but from how we treat others when no one is watching. Justice and loyalty illuminate the heart and build an unshakable foundation for a life guided by honor. Walk in truth, and the Creator will walk beside you.

Thirteenth Key to Unlock Your Blessing…

Discern your feelings of discomfort.

Discerning your feelings of discomfort and controlling your emotions and their effects is a significant way to unlock your blessings and expose the light of your path.

There are two categories of emotions: the fruit of the spirit and the vexations of your actions. Both types drive your existence, are a part of your past, and lead to your future events.

The Bible is one of the excellent sources that explains the first as, the fruit of the spirit is love, joy, peace, longsuffering, gentleness, goodness, faith, meekness, [and] temperance" (Galatians 5:22–23). The practice of the spiritual qualities and actions will unlock your blessings and lead to "goodness and righteousness and truth" (Ephesians 5:9). This alone will dispel all wrong thinking and guide you to your path.

Your emotions and your spirit will let you know when something is not correct. Quickly discern the feelings, find the root cause, and change your mindset, whether it requires forgiveness, dispelling unnecessary fear, or a general change in how you treat others. Do not let the sun set on your negative emotion.

The causes may be subtle and quickly dispellable, or they may be significant enough to lead to long-term sadness. Whatever the case, figure out a way to switch the emotion to a positive one. This may be difficult to practice; however, you will indeed be blessed. If you harbor any negative emotion for an extended period, you may be harmed by not fully processing your feelings, which will prevent all good from coming your way.

Vexations of our spirit are carried through negative emotions such as anger, emptiness, frustration, inadequacy, helplessness, fear, guilt, loneliness, depression, overwhelmed, failure, sadness, resentment, and jealousy. Quickly recognize this list of vexations and turn it around to concentrate on your fruit. This will keep you on your path of blessings.

You will be happy and satisfied in a state of joy and thankfulness. For the next 21 days, discern your feelings of discomfort. Change the feelings you have. Analyze each experience for 21 days. When the 21 days are over, meditate for the next 7 days on the entire 3 weeks to determine how you felt each day.

When you change your negative feelings into fruitfulness, you will feel a sense of weightlessness.

Author's Follow-Up (Reflection)

Through years of practice, I discovered that our moments of discomfort are sacred messengers, not punishments. They reveal what is unsettled within us and invite transformation. When I began to pause and truly listen to my discomfort rather than resist it, I found wisdom hidden inside what I once feared.

Discerning discomfort became a practice of spiritual honesty. I learned that negative emotions are not the enemy; they are indicators that I have drifted from peace. The more quickly I acknowledged them, the faster I could realign with my spirit. When anger or sadness visited, I asked, What lesson are you bringing me? Every answer led back to love, forgiveness, or release.

This practice reshaped my relationships, my patience, and my understanding of compassion. I became less reactive and more aware of the light within myself and others. Over time, my discomforts transformed into gentle reminders of growth rather than burdens of pain.

Now I see that each uneasy feeling is an opportunity to return to balance. When we face discomfort with awareness and gratitude, the Creator replaces pain with peace. In that stillness, blessings flow freely, and the heart feels light once again.

Fourteenth Key to Unlock Your Blessing…

Take action instead of reacting.

Do not react. Blessings will undoubtedly come from refraining from the reaction. Your reaction is an emotional, subconscious action based on the decision you make, and you do not consider any of the consequences. For you to unlock blessings, respond instead of reacting.

Responding requires a conscious effort to pause, review the emotions of the situation, and consider the appropriate action to take.

It may not be easy at first, but it gets easier with practice. You become aware of people's actions and how they affect your emotions, which require a response, and your blessings will come.

This pause and analysis will lead you to the correct path and guide you to consider danger or emotions, helping you make the right decisions.

Taking a moment to breathe can make all the difference, helping you avoid embarrassing moments or vexations that lead to other problems and situations.

If you find yourself reacting, stop immediately and evaluate the root cause that leads to your feelings. Use this hindsight to avoid future events that could block you from your blessings.

If we practice this and develop to where we always respond, we will recognize the fruits of the spirit and receive the many blessings coming our way.

Reacting may be quick and responding slow; however, responding takes more effort to learn, which creates a level of wisdom that will grow.

You will be happy and satisfied in a state of joy and thankfulness. For the next 21 days, respond instead of reacting. Pause and assess situations for your emotions and feelings. Analyze each experience for 21 days. When the 21 days are over, meditate for the next 7 days on the entire 3 weeks to determine how you felt each day.

When you learn how to respond and never react, you will feel a sense of weightlessness.

Author's Follow-Up (Reflection)

Looking back, this teaching, take action instead of reacting, has transformed my life in ways I never expected. Recently, I've come to understand that real strength lies not in the quickness of our reaction, but in the calmness of our spirit when we choose to pause. Every moment I've taken a breath before speaking, every time I've observed instead of defending, has created space for peace and clarity.

There were days I failed and reacted anyway, but even those moments became teachers. They reminded me that growth is not perfection, it's persistence. Responding invites divine order, allowing blessings to unfold in their time.

Now, I see that the pause between emotion and response is sacred. It's in that stillness that wisdom whispers and the Creator guides.

As I continue this practice, I feel lighter, more attuned to gratitude, more aware of the beauty in restraint. May we all walk this path together, responding with purpose, grace, and love, so that our blessings never miss their way to us.

Fifteenth Key to Unlock Your Blessing…

Be a light.

Be a light and be blessed. We often hear that we should be a light that shines; however, do you know how and what it means? There are many interpretations of this, and I will attempt to explain how this will unlock your blessings and lead you on your path to success.

We may see our world as dark, especially with the negative news and media. This negativity will harm our soul, spirit, and body as well as block our blessings.

"You are the light of the world. A city that is set on a hill cannot be hidden. Nor do they light a lamp and put it under a basket, but on a lampstand, and it gives light to all who are in the house. Let your light so shine before men, that they may see your good works and glorify your Father in heaven." (Matthew 5:14-16)

If we let darkness surround us, we will be consumed by it. If we shine our light, we push back on this darkness. We accomplish this with the fruits of the Spirit mentioned in Galatians chapter 5, "But the fruit of the Spirit is love, joy, peace, patience, kindness, goodness, faithfulness, gentleness, and self-control."

Practicing these virtues will equip you with a pleasing personality, and your light will shine so bright as to attract all blessings, shine on your path, and inspire others.

Just as natural light is used for our directional purpose, your internal light will guide you and others around you out of darkness and clarify situations and surroundings.

If you let your light shine, you will pierce the darkness and unlock the floodgates of blessings that are coming your way. You will draw pleasant and like-minded people to you, and they will naturally be drawn to you. People will notice what you have and want the same thing. You will be an inspiration and blessing to all those who surround you. Be a light and be blessed.

You will be happy and satisfied in a state of joy and thankfulness. For the next 21 days, be a light. Shine for all. Analyze each experience for 21 days. When the 21 days are over, meditate for the next 7 days on the entire 3 weeks to determine how you felt each day.

When you become a light, you will feel a sense of weightlessness.

Author's Follow-Up (Reflection)

In reflecting on this teaching, Be a Light, I have come to understand that being a light is not about perfection or constant positivity. It is about presence. It is choosing to illuminate rather than absorb the darkness that surrounds us. Recently, I've seen how one kind word, one patient act, or one moment of forgiveness can shift the energy in a room and open the door for blessings to flow.

There were times when I felt dimly overwhelmed by negativity or burdened by the world's heaviness. Yet, I learned that even the smallest light still shines in darkness. When I returned to love, joy, and gentleness, the glow reignited within me.

Being a light means standing firm in faith and radiating peace when others lose hope. It is walking as an example of the Creator's goodness, guiding others not with words but with consistent actions of love.

Today, I strive to keep my lamp burning. Each day, I choose light over fear, gratitude over complaint, compassion over anger, and I see blessings multiply. May your light never fade; may it continue to guide, heal, and reveal the beauty of your path.

Sixteenth Key to Unlock Your Blessing...

Use appropriate words.

Use appropriate words, and the blessings you give shall be returned to you again. We have all heard the saying, Do not say anything unless you have something positive to say.

Well, you need to take this to heart. Not only should you not speak negatively, but you should also not entertain it in your imagination. Negative words will have a long-lasting result that spreads far beyond the person to whom you speak. Words are powerful. They embed themselves in the mind. Words are sound frequencies that describe the inner feeling of the individual.

This verse is a powerful example; O generation of vipers, how can ye, being evil, speak good things? for out of the abundance of the heart the mouth speaketh. A good man out of the good treasure of the heart bringeth forth good things: and an evil man out of the evil treasure bringeth forth evil things. But I say unto you, That every idle word that men shall speak, they shall give account thereof in the day of judgment. For by thy words thou shalt be justified, and by thy words thou shalt be condemned. Mathew 12:34-37

We should always edify each other, as this will lead to blessings.

This is another biblical principle; oikodomé, which translates as "the building of a house." We build up by using our words and tear down by doing the same. If we expect to be blessed, then we must first give the blessings.

It is no mystery that we use spelling to mean putting together phonetic symbols to produce a sound. We are casting a spell each time we speak. This book makes you imagine the words and repeat them in your mind, entering both your conscious and subconscious mind. These words will eventually become a part of your thinking and then become you.

If you use or listen to negative words or curses, you are imposing a wish of evil against another; to imprecate evil upon them; to call for mischief or injury to fall upon them; to execrate them. This will reap the same, block all blessings, and dim the light to your path.

You will be happy and satisfied in a state of joy and thankfulness. For the next 21 days, use appropriate words. Analyze each experience for 21 days. When the 21 days are over, meditate for the next 7 days on the entire 3 weeks to determine how you felt each day.

When you use appropriate words, you will feel a sense of weightlessness.

Author's Follow-Up (Reflection)

Reflecting on using appropriate words, I have come to recognize even more deeply the creative power that lives within the tongue. Words are not merely sounds; they are seeds. They take root in the hearts of those who hear them and grow into thoughts, emotions, and actions. I have learned that the blessings or burdens in my life often trace back to what I have spoken aloud or allowed to live in my mind.

Throughout this past year, I have witnessed how a kind word can heal, while careless speech can wound beyond measure. Speaking of life, encouragement, and truth, even in difficult moments, has opened doors to peace and opportunities I never expected. The more I disciplined my tongue, the more I noticed harmony and grace flowing into my relationships and work.

This reflection has taught me that blessing others through language is akin to building a world of light around you. The vibration of your words sets the tone for your path. Speak with intention. Choose words that uplift, restore, and align with goodness, and you will continue to unlock blessings that return to you in overflowing measure.

Seventeenth Key to Unlock Your Blessing…

Control imagination.

Controlling your imagination is a significant part of unlocking your blessings. All things are created first in your imagination. You are constantly planning, even if you are unaware. Everything is born as a thought, and through meditation and imagination, we take baby steps that lead to our path and blessings. The Creator has blessed you with a mind to create through your imagination.

You cannot manipulate your life to become the Creator, but we can participate by using our imagination for our blessings.

You can use your imagination to diminish and eliminate the perception of your obstacles and dilemmas. When your imagination and excitement are combined, you will notice that barriers will subside quickly. Your blessings will run over where you have no room to receive them. This will lead you to more imagination, inspiration, and courage.

Imagination is often encouraged by life experiences and the things you are exposed to. If you need inspiration, you can converse with like-minded people and read inspirational books or movies.

When you use your imagination, your mind expands. It is just like a muscle; it increases. You can activate your brain by practicing daily and being aware of your conscious imagination. Use your imagination often, and as your imagination muscle strengthens, blessings will blossom.

The best way to control your imagination is by concentrating on the end or result. Have a clear picture of the results, and you will begin to take baby steps toward your goals. Your blessings will manifest, and the light will shine on your path.

You will be happy and satisfied in a state of joy and thankfulness. For the next 21 days, control your imagination. Exercise thinking about the result.

Analyze each experience for 21 days. When the 21 days are over, meditate for the next 7 days on the entire 3 weeks to determine how you felt each day.

When you control your imagination, you will feel a sense of weightlessness.

Author's Follow-Up (Reflection)

Reflecting on control of imagination now, I have learned that imagination is both a sacred tool and a powerful responsibility. What we allow to live in our minds eventually takes form in our reality. Every vision, word, and emotion we nurture within our inner world becomes a seed for what will appear in our outer world.

These past years, I realized how easily the mind can wander into fear, doubt, or limitation when it is left unchecked. But when I consciously directed my imagination toward faith, gratitude, and purpose, I saw miracles unfold, sometimes quietly, sometimes in ways too powerful to ignore. The imagination is the bridge between prayer and manifestation; it is the language through which we communicate our trust in the Creator.

By focusing on positive outcomes and releasing the temptation to dwell on obstacles, I have witnessed blessings flow more freely. The more I disciplined my imagination, the more clarity and peace I gained. To control imagination is not to suppress creativity, but to align it with light and truth. When your inner vision is rooted in goodness, your path will always be illuminated, and your blessings will multiply.

Eighteenth Key to Unlock Your Blessing…

Do not gossip.

Do not gossip. Gossiping will block your blessings, and you will not be able to see the light that shines on your path.

When you gossip, you will be vexed with consequences, temporarily making you feel superior to the person you are gossiping about. Then the pendulum swings to the opposite, making you feel inferior to everyone. You are showing that you need validation for your actions. It is a vicious cycle and hard to break.

When you steal another person's reputation by spreading rumors and gossiping, you also show who you are to the person you are gossiping to. This person may listen; however, they will never trust you. Resist all temptation to gossip, and you will be blessed. Do not concern yourself if the story is true or not; it has nothing to do with you.

When you gossip, you form opinions about a person, altering your viewpoint based on someone else without facts. You block essential conversations that you may otherwise have that would lead you to your blessings or the path you would take.

If you are approached by gossip, you can quickly change the conversation into something positive about a meaningful subject.

It is unnecessary to make the gossiper feel uncomfortable; however, you cannot feed into the discussion. There is no need to repeat the gossip; why would you if it has nothing to do with you?

You will be blessed if you practice not gossiping. Never judge others based on things you hear and think before you speak. Remember, you are showing who you really are when you gossip.

Finally, be mindful of the people you keep company with, if they gossip. They will gossip about you, and your blessings will be blocked. Do not gossip, and you will be blessed.

You will be happy and satisfied in a state of joy and thankfulness. For the next 21 days, do not gossip. Analyze each experience for 21 days. When the 21 days are over, meditate for the next 7 days on the entire 3 weeks to determine how you felt each day.

When you do not gossip, you will feel a sense of weightlessness.

Author's Follow-Up (Reflection)

This key, do not gossip; it rings truer than ever. The world feels louder now, filled with voices eager to share opinions, assumptions, and fragments of truth. Yet through experience, I have learned that gossip carries a heavy vibration; it drains spiritual energy. It clouds the light meant to guide us. Each careless word spreads ripples that return to us in ways we may not expect.

Choosing silence over gossip is not weakness; it is mastery. It takes strength to hold your tongue when others speak carelessly and even more strength to redirect a conversation toward goodness. Over time, I've seen that refraining from gossip attracts peace, trust, and respect. People begin to sense your integrity, and blessings flow where judgment once stood.

I now recognize that gossip not only harms others but also fractures our own spirit. When we honor others' dignity in their absence, we are also celebrating the divine within ourselves. In a world quick to speak, may we become those who listen, reflect, and uplift. When our words carry light, truth, and compassion, our blessings expand beyond measure, and the weight of negativity fades into nothingness.

Nineteenth Key to Unlock Your Blessing…

Have faith even in darkness.

Having faith even in darkness is a powerful way to unlock blessings. It is easy to have faith when we see the situation going well, but we must increase our confidence when we do not know. Blessed are those who have not seen and yet have believed" (John 20:29). The light shines bright in the darkness; the light pierces the darkness. If we have faith in the things not seen, our blessings will be great. We have a little light that shines on the path of our feet. We take baby steps each day, relying solely on our faith that we are doing what we are meant to do.

Faith is the light and power through the unseen. It breaks down obstacles, gives us hope, and strengthens our beliefs and imaginations. We will witness our blessings and those of those who are with us.

A lack of faith will allow your circumstances to steal your blessings. Your feelings will take over and close your eyes to your path. You could be in a fight-or-flight thought process when situations arise if you do not have faith.

Having faith will unlock your blessings.

Faith in darkness helps us control our imagination to stay positive even in uncertain times. When you have doubt, pray, or meditate on the results that you desire. Be sincere and enthusiastic in believing that what you ask, you have already received. With this practice, you will unlock the floodgates of blessings and indeed see the light on your path.

You will be happy and satisfied in a state of joy and thankfulness. For the next 21 days, have faith even in darkness. See the light that pierces the darkness for 21 days.

When the 21 days are over, meditate for the next 7 days on the entire 3 weeks to determine how you felt each day.

When you have unwavering faith, you will feel a sense of weightlessness.

Author's Follow-Up (Reflection)

Faith in darkness has carried me through more than I could have imagined. In moments when answers seemed distant and the path unclear, I found that faith was not about sight; it was about surrender. The unseen became my teacher. Each trial revealed a lesson: that true faith glows most brightly when there is no visible light to guide you.

Over the past year, I have learned that faith is an act of courage. It asks us to move forward when logic says stand still, to trust that each step is guided, even when we cannot see the ground beneath our feet. The blessings that follow such faith are not always immediate, but they are always sure.

Faith in darkness transforms fear into strength and uncertainty into opportunity. It reminds us that the Creator's hand is steady, even when we tremble. Every time we choose belief over doubt, the light within grows stronger, and the darkness loses its power.

Hold faith close in every storm, and you will find peace in the unseen. When you trust that blessings are forming even in shadow, your spirit will rise, and you will feel the beautiful, freeing weightlessness of divine assurance.

Twentieth Key to Unlock Your Blessing…
Define your ultimate purpose.

Defining your ultimate purpose is your primary goal in life. Unlocking your blessings is the way to determine your purpose. When you train yourself to unlock blessings by fixing little habits, you will be able to figure out what you like to do. Finding our ultimate purpose can be challenging, but there are ways to help you decide. It could be from your passions or talents, or just by accident.

Getting to the root cause of obstacles is one of the most transparent ways to define your purpose. You will be able to block pressures from others who do not understand what makes you. By following this method, you will find your true calling and know that you are on the correct lighted path of blessings.

One of the ways to explore your purpose is to define what you love to do. Does it come easily? Do you not get bored or tired? Has this been a dream for a long time? Chances are, this is your purpose. When you define this, you will need to develop your talents and engage your family and friends.

It is a good idea to write your purpose down on paper. Read it and change it until it is perfect. Meditate on it daily, repeat the words often, keep it with you, make a vision board, etc. Each exercise will bring this closer to fruition.

When you discover your ultimate purpose, the blessings will flow through you, and you will be a blessing to all that you encounter.

You will be happy and satisfied in a state of joy and thankfulness. For the next 21 days, define your ultimate purpose. When the 21 days are over, meditate for the next 7 days on the entire 3 weeks to determine how you felt each day.

When you have defined your purpose, you will feel a sense of weightlessness.

Author's Follow-Up (Reflection)

Purpose is no longer something I search for—it is something I live. Through these past few years, I've come to understand that defining one's ultimate purpose is not a single revelation but a continuous unfolding. It evolves as we do. What once felt like a distant calling has become a daily practice of listening to the quiet voice within, the one that whispers truth when the world is loud.

My purpose has deepened with service, compassion, and courage. It is not just about what I do but who I am becoming through it. I've learned that purpose is not found in perfection or accomplishment, but in alignment, when your heart, actions, and faith move together in harmony.

Defining purpose requires stillness, honesty, and willingness to grow beyond comfort. Each act of clarity brings blessings that confirm you are walking the right path. When we align with divine intent, life begins to flow with grace rather than struggle.

Live your purpose with gratitude and trust. When your purpose is rooted in love and guided by spirit, every step becomes sacred. The path ahead glows brighter, and you feel that gentle, unmistakable sense of weightlessness, knowing you are exactly where you are meant to be.

Individual Coincidence

It's a coincidence; you are an individual.

Your intention resulted from your attention

in cooperation with the indivisible.

This led you to your production

which is a coincidence.

Your attention led to your intention

to cooperate with the indivisible.

This led you to your destruction

which is a coincidence,

you are an individual

in cooperation with the indivisible.

Your attention will always guide you

to your intention, this must be,

in cooperation with the indivisible,

to bring you your production or destruction

for you are an individual.

You are intentional and coincidental

An individual in cooperation with the indivisible.

Tyrese Gould Jacinto 2021

Author's Poem Explanation

You are an individual, yet that individuality doesn't stand alone. Your attention (where you place your focus) and your intention (what you aim to create) are not purely personal acts; they happen in cooperation with the indivisible, the divine reality or creative force that underlies all.

When your attention aligns with divine cooperation, it leads to production, bringing forth blessings, creativity, and growth. But if your attention or intention strays from that harmonious cooperation, it can lead to destruction, loss, pain, and disconnection. Both outcomes are "coincidences" because they arise from this sacred interplay, not by accident.

Thus, you embody paradox: you are in-tentional yet co-incidental, you act with purpose but always within a cosmic weave you share with the Creator. You are an indivi-dual in co-operation with the indi-visible, a unique expression bound to the infinite.

In short, your inner focus shapes your outer world, and both are always happening together with the Creator, through you.

Acknowledgement

I realize how blessed I am in the mere fact that my husband, father, and children are enlightened souls.

I felt such a tremendous loss when my grandmother, Marion, passed; she and I would have long conversations about enlightenment.

Little did I realize that my children were always listening. I have gained a deep understanding from my children and know that my grandmother continues because of them.

My husband, Victor, is wise beyond anyone's knowledge. His experiences and insight into life are unique. He sees things clearly and does not hold back when it comes to voicing his wisdom to me.

My father, Mark, is a wise soul and sometimes makes you think he is unaware, but he is not. My Dad lets me speak, listens intensely, and makes me feel like I know something, even though he already knows the answer.

I acknowledge you all and thank the Creator for allowing me to be a part of you.

www.ingramcontent.com/pod-product-compliance
Lightning Source LLC
Chambersburg PA
CBHW040940100426
42812CB00016B/2631